Infection Control
in the Natural and Spiritual

Infection Control
in the Natural and Spiritual

Shera Ynez Smith

J. Kenkade
PUBLISHING®
LITTLE ROCK, ARKANSAS

Infection Control in the Natural and Spiritual
Copyright © 2021 by Shera Ynez Smith

J. Kenkade Publishing
6104 Forbing Rd
Little Rock, AR 72209
www.jkenkade.com
Facebook.com/JKenkade

J. Kenkade Publishing is a registered trademark.

Printed in the United States of America
ISBN 978-1-955186-06-3

Unless otherwise noted, scripture quotations are taken from the King James Version® Bible, Public Domain.

Table of Contents

Chapter 1

✝

THE NATURAL
AND THE SPIRITUAL

Some of you wouldn't believe me if I told you that we are spiritual beings having natural experiences. We are, though. Everything we go through in life has a purpose, whether it be something that was planned, self-inflicted, or just plain coincidental. It is all for our greater good.

Now, let's talk about the natural and spiritual sides of things. Well, we'll start with us—meaning ourselves, me and you. The individual who stands before you in the mirror from day to day. That's if you ever even look in a mirror. Some of us don't really take the time to actually look at ourselves and see who is staring back at us. When you do look at the image before you, do you see yourself or Christ?

Just know that the individual who stands before you has two sides to them:

1. Natural (carnal) side, which is the flesh that we live in, according to the Bible.

2. Spiritual side, described as the "spiritual" in the Bible.

Let's go a bit further and break "natural" and "spiritual" down as they relate to what we are talking about here:

1. Natural– Being in a state of nature without spiritual enlightenment.

2. Spiritual– Relating to or affecting the human spirit or soul as opposed to material or physical things.

Spiritual Being: an incorporeal (not composed of matter; having no material existence) being believed to have the power to affect the course of human events.

Now that we have a breakdown of what these two things are, we can move forward with how to understand our individual selves better with this bit of knowledge and some spiritual truth. We have to go to the book of Genesis and truly start at the beginning when God made Man.

We'll start with the creation of Man in Genesis 1:26, "And God said, Let us make man in our image, after our likeness…"

This is where we can see God as a spiritual being Himself, along with Jesus and the Holy Spirit causing natural things to occur according to John 1:1, "In the beginning was the Word…"

We see where God did several things here before Man became flesh or a "natural" human being.

The first thing God did was speak.

See, one thing we have to realize is the fact that we are spiritual beings. You can speak a thing, and it shall come to pass according to your faith. Isaiah 55:11 says, "So shall my word be that goeth forth out of my mouth…"

Next, God created in Genesis 27.

When something is created, it is being brought into existence. I see God here visualizing Man in His image, utilizing every aspect of His being to make a male or female to take care of this earth the way He would take care of it.

Then, if we look in Genesis 28, we see that He blessed them "to be fruitful and multiply, and replenish the earth, and subdue it." God had big plans for Man at this time and apparently looked forward to them being followed through the way He planned. But we have to know that because God is God, He has a plan within a plan. Just know He is the Plan.

Finally, we get to see God's vision of His image coming forth. Let's move on to chapter 2 in Genesis where we see a miracle performed before our eyes. Verse 6 refers to a mist going "up from the earth…". Verse 7 says, "And the Lord God formed man of the dust of the ground, and breathed into his nostrils the breath of life; and man became a living soul."

This was the last thing God did here. He "breathed" life into His creation, which was blessed before the manifestation, created in His image, and spoken into existence before the manifestation actually took place.

This is where we start to understand what it means to be a spiritual being having natural experiences. It started with God first, then Jesus. But why wouldn't it? He is the Creator of all things right.

Chapter 2

✝

WHAT ARE YOU MADE OF?

When we look at the creation of Man, we see what all was involved in creating God's image in His likeness. Genesis 2:7 says, "And the Lord God formed man of the dust of the ground, and breathed into his nostrils the breath of life; and man became a living soul."

In this scripture alone, this one thing stands out: "the dust of the ground". Now, when I see this, I think "dirt" and that this dirt came from the ground. Let's remember we are talking about infection control, so just know you can have an infected ground, tainted soil, or trash in your dirt. But this was in the beginning, so no soil was tainted at this time. Everything was pure.

And this is what we were created from: dust.

Naturally, let's take a closer look at "dust" – or "dirt" for that matter. If we were to look at dust or dirt underneath a microscope, it may look like tiny particles on a slide. It could be good or bad. If it is bad, it will appear different and react differently than the good dirt or dust.

See, before the fall of Man, everything was perfect. The relationship God had with His creation was perfect. The world was perfect. At this point, Man was spoken into existence and then manifested out in the open according to scripture. I can see us being totally spiritual beings in natural bodies created from the dust of the ground because of the image that God imagined that was blessed to carry the breath of God to survive off of. Just perfect, right?

After the fall of Man in Genesis 3 is when the "dust of the ground" becomes tainted. Because of the disobedience of the one created, all hell breaks loose. Instantly, Adam and Eve recognize themselves as being unclothed or naked. They feel the need to cover themselves in verse 7. At this point, their relationship with God is broken. If you read chapter 3 in the text, you will see what transpired to cause the broken relationship with God.

Now, let's go back to that dust or dirt. Spiritually, our dirt can be pure, or it can be tainted. As humans were spiritual beings before the fall, of course everything was perfect. But after the fall, we see things like fear, pride, doubt, shame, and blame reflected in their actions. A number of things happened due to temptation.

Now there are a lot of things that can taint the dirt, and there are a lot of things that can clean it up. This is why it's important to know what you are made of and recognize if your own dust or dirt/flesh is tainted or pure. Remember: nobody is perfect, but there are ways to clean and disinfect our dust or dirt/flesh. Understand that this is how the original man was made, strictly from "the dust of the ground".

Chapter 3

✝

The Vessel

If you know anything about vessels, most are made from clay or dirt. Some vessels are made with pure dirt, and some are made of tainted clay.

We will look at the comparison between the clay/vessel itself and the natural/human vessel.

Let's see what a vessel and clay really are:

1. VESSEL: a hollow container, especially one used to hold liquid, such as a bowl or cask or (chiefly in or alluding to biblical use) a person, especially regarded as holding or embodying a particular quality.

2. CLAY: a fine-grained silicate mineral made when rocks break down. Wet clay is soft and can be shaped to make pottery, bricks, and other things. When it is shaped and then fired in a kiln

to make it hard, it becomes pottery. Clay often contains some water because the water molecules stick to the tiny grains.

Now that we have a better understanding of the vessel and the clay, let's see how the two relate naturally and spiritually. We will see how infection control is involved.

With a clay vessel, we must use water to mold it and shape it into the image that it was envisioned to create. You can make a bowl, vase, or cup. Whatever you choose. Once it has set and dried, it becomes a household favorite to use often or not at all. Now, if that item gets dirty or broken, there's a process of infection control that should take place. This process involves cleaning, sanitizing, and disinfecting.

When the human vessel is formed in Genesis 2:6-7, we see where water has been used to form Man from the dust or dirt of the ground. God strategically formed Man in His image and in His likeness to be just like Him, perfect (without flaw) and used for God's glory. But an inclination to sin, which is known as temptation, shows up and attaches itself to the human vessel and causes sin to take place. This is how the infestation of sin starts. From this point, the human vessel is tainted, flawed, contaminated, and sometimes broken. There's a process of infection control that should also take place here. This process involves repenting, being born again, and being filled with the Holy Spirit.

Now that we have taken a look at the vessel naturally and spiritually/clay or human, we can move forward with discussing the broken vessel or anything that has negatively impacted the vessel's relationship with the Creator.

Chapter 4

✝

THE BROKEN VESSEL

A vessel can be very delicate or hardcore. It just depends on how it's made and what it is made of. And depending how it is taken care of or treated, it can end up broken one way or another. We'll address the broken vessel from natural and spiritual standpoints here as well.

Let's start with that broken vessel on the natural side. As stated earlier, it depends on how it is made and what it is made of that dictate its stability and longevity. But it also depends on how it is handled in certain situations, and that determines if it will stay whole or not.

It's the same in the spiritual. Depending on what is poured into that vessel, it can cause a reaction that can be detrimental to the stability of the vessel.

Okay, I'll go a little deeper.

Imagine a pretty, clear vase with roses in it that are beautiful and captivating to the eye. If you don't change the water, the roses die, and the vessel gets nasty on the inside and possibly on the outside. It all depends on how it is taken care of and what it is specifically used for. I know that clay or glass vessels have all sorts of purposes. What matter most are how useful that vessel can be and for how long before it deteriorates or is even broken.

Now, let's flip it.

We as human vessels carry a lot spiritually, physically, mentally, emotionally, and financially. We really don't know how much power we possess through Jesus Christ. Now, without Jesus, all those areas that I mentioned earlier can be handled when we realize that God/Jesus is the Potter and we are the clay.

It is up to us to allow God to mold and transform us from the inside out the way He sees fit for us to be. Romans 12:2 says it well: "And be not conformed to this world: but be ye transformed by the renewing of your mind, that ye may prove what is that good, and acceptable, and perfect, will of God."

As an individual who has been broken into many pieces, I have to know that there is a way to be restored and be made like new. It takes an open heart and mind to allow God to come in and take those broken pieces, dust them off, clean them up, and put them back together again. It's better to let God restore than Man because God knows just what it takes to keep it all together.

Chapter 5

✝

THE VESSEL RESTORED

At this point, I hope we have a clearer understanding of the title of this book. I hope you understand yourself to be a vessel that in the beginning of time was created from the dust of the ground to molded and shaped– better yet formed– into the image and likeness of God. This is where the formed vessel was made perfect but later tainted with sin and shame through the beguiling of the serpent.

Genesis 3:13 says, "But God…"

We have a Redeemer. As spiritual beings born into sinful flesh, when we are old enough and taught the knowledge of Jesus Christ, we can be saved, healed, and delivered from the bondage of sin and shame.

Ephesians 1:7 says "In him we have redemption through His blood…"

It's the blood of Jesus that cleanses and restores that broken vessel.

1 John 1:7-10 says, "And the blood of Jesus Christ his Son cleanseth us for all sin…"

In order to practice proper infection control in your life, you must be able and willing to follow simple instructions. These instructions are from the Holy Bible. I know no other book that was designed as a personal handbook for living. That's just what the Bible is: Basic Instructions Before Leaving Earth.

Knowing the ABCs for salvation will help also:

A- **Admit** you are a sinner and have made mistakes.

B- **Believe** that Jesus is God's Son, die on the Cross for you, and rose up from the grave on the third day.

C- **Confess** Jesus as the Lord of your life and **commit** yourself to a life of following Jesus and serving others.

The cleansing process is simple when it is desired wholeheartedly. I pray that the vessel reading this book is blessed beyond measure for there is more to come involving infection control.

Infection Control
in the Natural and Spiritual:
Workbook

CHAPTER 1
The Natural and The Spiritual

Have you ever been feeling a certain way and then when you actually look at yourself in the mirror, you don't look as bad as you feel?

Exercise:

Find a mirror wherever you are. Take a moment and take a look in that mirror. What do you see? Who do you see? Naturally or spiritually, what do you see?

1. Define "natural" according to the text.

_____
_____
_____
_____

2. Define "spiritual" according to the text.

_____
_____
_____
_____

Now knowing that each individual has two sides to them, let's get a deeper understanding as an individual regarding both sides.

A spiritual being is...

_____

_____

_____

_____

With this bit of knowledge, moving forward should be an easy task. It requires effort, commitment, hunger, and desire to know more from this point. I say it should be an easy task because this will require you to pull out your Bible or the Bible app, whichever one you choose, but it will be needed in order to go on with the remainder of the workbook. The information given, of course, goes along with your book. But what happens often is that we just read the book and never take the time to see if the author is telling the truth or sharing mistruths. You may also wonder why there is so much reading and writing to answer that question. Repetition is a key factor to get the proper spiritual cleansing and deliverance needed when wanting to be better. Now, we can move forward with how to understand our individual selves better with this bit of knowledge and some spiritual truth.

Let's go to the book of Genesis and start at the beginning when God made man. We'll start with reading the Creation of Man in Genesis 1:26-27.

_____

_____

_____

_____

_____

_____

_____

_____

_____

_____

This is where we can see God as a spiritual being Himself, along with Jesus and the Holy Spirit causing natural things to occur according to John 1:1-3.

We'll see how the Old Testament and New Testament work together as well during this study.

Let's read John 1:1-3.

_____

_____

_____

_____

_____

_____

_____

This would be a great time to go back to the beginning of the book of Genesis and catch up on the full aspect of the creation and how God, being a spiritual being, spoke those things into existence. See, one thing we have to realize is the fact that we are spiritual beings. We can speak a thing, and it shall come to pass according to our faith in Isaiah 55:11.

Let's read Isaiah 55:11.

_____

_____

_____

_____

_____

Next, let's read and see where God Created in Genesis 1:27.

_____

_____

_____

_____

_____

_____

_____

_____

When something is created, what is happening to it?

_____

_____

_____

_____

_____

At this point, I see God here visualizing Man in His image, utilizing every aspect of His being to make a male or female to take care of this earth the way He would take care of it. Then, if we go on to read in verse 28, we see that He blessed them "to be fruitful and multiply, and replenish the earth, and subdue it." God had big plans for Man at this time and apparently looked forward to them being followed through the way He intended. But we have to know that because God is God, He has a plan within a plan. Just know He is the Plan. Finally, we get to see God's vision for His image coming forth. Stop here to read chapter 2 in Genesis. Life changes for man at this very moment, and this is where we see a miracle performed before our eyes. Verse 6 refers to a mist going "up from the earth", and verse 7 says, "...and the Lord God formed man of the dust of the ground, and breathed into his nostrils the breath of life; and man became a living soul." This was the last thing God did here. He "breathed" life into His creation, which was blessed before the manifestation, created in His image and spoken into existence before the manifestation actually took place.

This is where we start in understanding what it means to be spiritual beings having natural experiences. It started with God first, then Jesus. But why wouldn't it? He is the creator of all things right.

Scripture:

"For this cause we also, since the day we heard it, do not cease to pray for you, and to desire that ye might be filled with the knowledge of his will in all wisdom and spiritual understanding..."
Colossians 1:9

Prayer:

Heavenly Father,

Thank you for helping me to understand who I really am, to whom I belong, and how to be better. Continue to lead and guide me along the way so I can be a better me for you.

In Jesus' name. Amen.

CHAPTER 2
What Are You Made Of?

"From ashes to ashes, from dust to dust" is a saying used during burial services in reference to committing one's body to the ground. Ever thought about how all those years ago God created Man from the very ground we are put in after we leave this life spiritually?

When we look at the creation of Man, we can see what all was involved in creating us in God's likeness. Genesis 2:7 says,

_____
_____
_____
_____
_____
_____
_____

In this scripture alone, this one thing stands out: "the _____ of the ground". Now, this dirt came from the ground. Let's remember we are talking about infection control, so just know you can have an infected ground, tainted soil, or trash in your dirt. But this was in the beginning, so no soil was tainted at this time. Everything was pure. And this is what we were created from: dust. Naturally, let's take a closer look at "dust"– or "dirt" for that matter. If we were to look at dust or dirt underneath a microscope, it may look like tiny particles on a slide. It could be good or bad. If it is bad, it will appear different and react differently than good dirt or dust.

See, before the fall of Man, everything was perfect. The _____ God had

    A) religion   B) love
    C) relationship   D) friendship

with His creation was perfect. The world was perfect. At this point, Man was spoken into existence and then manifested out in the open according to scripture. I can see us being totally spiritual beings in natural bodies created from the dust of the ground because of the image that God had that was blessed to carry the breath of God to survive off of. Just perfect, right? After the fall of Man in Genesis 3, this is when the "dust of the ground" becomes tainted. Because of the _____ of the one created, all hell breaks loose. Instantly, Adam and Eve recognized that they were not clothed or naked. They felt the need to cover themselves is as seen in Genesis 3:7. _____

_____

_____

_____

_____

At this point, the relationship with God has been broken. If you read Chapter 3 in the text, you will see what transpired to cause the broken relationship with God.

Now, let's go back to that dust or dirt. Spiritually, our dirt can be pure, or it can be tainted. As a _____ before the fall, of course everything was _____. But after the fall, we see things like _____ _____. A number of things happened due to temptation. Now, there are a lot of things that can taint the dirt, and there are a lot of things that can clean it up. This is why it's important to know what you are made of and recognize if your own "dust" or "dirt"– your flesh– is tainted or pure. Remember: nobody is perfect, but there are ways to clean and disinfect our flesh. Understand that this is how the original man was made, strictly from "_____".

Scripture:

"Wash me thoroughly from mine iniquity, and cleanse me from my sin."
Psalms 51:2

Prayer:

Heavenly Father,

I know my flesh is weak, but my spirit is willing. You know what is in me that is not like You. Cleanse me, dear God. Make me as white as snow. In the process, teach me more of You so I can be the vessel You use.

In Jesus' name. Amen.

CHAPTER 3
The Vessel

If you know anything about vessels, you know that most are made from clay or dirt. Some vessels are made with pure dirt, and some are made of tainted clays.

We will look at the comparison of the clay/vessel itself and the natural/human vessel. Let's see what a vessel and clay really are. What is the difference between the vessel and clay?

1.   VESSEL: _____

_____

_____

_____

_____

2.   CLAY: _____

_____

_____

_____

_____

Now that we have a better understanding of the vessel and the clay, let's see how the two relate naturally and spiritually. We will also see how infection control is involved.

With a clay vessel, we must use

A) dirt   B) oil   C) water

to mold it and shape it into the image that it was envisioned to create. You can make a bowl, vase, or cup. Whatever you choose. Once it has set and dried, it becomes a household favorite to use often or not at all. Now, if that item gets dirty or broken, there's a process of infection control that should take place. This process involves

_____.

What was formed in Genesis 2:6-7 and what was used to form man from the dust or dirt of the ground?

_____

God _____ formed Man in _____ to be just like Him, perfect (without flaw) and used for _____. But an inclination to sin, which is known as _____, showed up and attached itself to the human vessel and caused sin to take place. This is how the infestation of sin started. From that point, the human vessel was tainted, flawed, contaminated, and sometimes broken. There's a process of infection control that should also take place here.

This process involves _____

_____

_____

_____

_____.

Now that we have taken a look at the vessel naturally and spiritually– the clay being a human– we can move forward with the broken vessel or anything that has negatively impacted the vessel's relationship with the Creator.

Scripture:

"What? know ye not that your body is the temple of the Holy Ghost which is in you, which ye have of God, and ye are not your own?"
1 Corinthians 6:19

Prayer:

Heavenly Father,

Help me to know that my body is not my own. Help me to keep it holy and sacred unto You. Cleanse me, purify me, pour your Holy Spirit into me so I can be a better me for You, Lord.

In Jesus' name. Amen.

CHAPTER 4
The Broken Vessel

_____ can be very _____ or _____. It just depends on how it's made and what it is made of. Depending how it is _____ of or _____, it can end up _____ one way or another. We'll address the broken vessel from natural and spiritual standpoints here as well.

We'll start with that broken vessel on the natural side. As stated earlier, it depends on how it is _____ and _____ it is made of that dictate its _____ and _____. But it also depends on how it is handled in certain situations, and that determines if it will stay whole or not.

It's the same in the spiritual. Depending on what is poured into that vessel, it can ____ _____ _____. Okay, I'll go a little deeper.

Imagine a pretty, clear vase with roses in it that are beautiful and captivating to the eye. If you don't _____, the roses _____, and

the vessel _____ on the _____
_____. It all depends on how
it is _____ and what it is _____. I
know that clay or glass vessels have all sorts of
_____. What matter most are _____
_____
_____ before it _____.

Now let's flip it.

We as human vessels carry a lot, _____
_____. We really
don't know how much _____ we possess
through_____.Now,withJesus,allthose
areas that I mentioned earlier can be _____
when we _____
_____.
It is up to us to allow God to_____
_____.

Romans 12:2 says, _____
_____
_____
_____
_____
_____.

As an individual who has been broken into many
pieces, I have to know that there is a way to be

_____and be made like _____. It takes an open _____and _____ to allow God to come in and take those broken pieces, dust them off, clean them up, and put them back together again. It's better to let God restore than Man because God knows just what it takes to keep it all together.

Scripture:

"The LORD is nigh unto them that are of a broken heart; and saveth such as be of a contrite spirit."
Psalms 34:18

Prayer:

Heavenly Father,

I've been broken, battered, and abused. Make me, mold me, and shape me, God. Put these broken pieces of me back together as only You know how. I trust You as my Creator to do Your will with me.

In Jesus' name. Amen.

CHAPTER 5
The Vessel Restored

At this point, I hope we have a clearer understanding of the title of this book. I hope you understand yourself to be a vessel that was created in the beginning of time _____ to be molded and shaped – better yet formed – into

   A) yourself   B) His likeness and His image
   C) Jesus   D) the Father.

This is where the formed vessel was made perfect but later tainted with sin and shame through the_____.

Genesis 3:13 says, "But God..."

We have a Redeemer. As spiritual beings born into sinful flesh, when we are old enough and taught the knowledge of Jesus Christ, we can be   _____.
Ephesians 1:7 says,

_____
_____
_____
_____

It's the_____ that _____ that broken vessel.

1 John 1:7-10 says, _____

_____

_____

_____

_____

_____

_____

_____

In order to practice proper infection control in your life, you must be able and willing to follow simple instructions. These instructions are from the _____. I know no other book that was designed as a personal handbook for living. That's just what the Bible is: Basic Instructions Before Leaving Earth.

Knowing the ABCs for salvation will help also:

A- _____
B- _____
C- _____
and **commit** yourself to a life of following Jesus and serving others.

Scripture:

"For I will restore health unto thee, and I will heal thee of thy wounds, saith the Lord; because they called thee an Outcast, saying, This is Zion, whom no man seeketh after."

Prayer:

Heavenly Father,

Help me be the restored vessel You have called me to be. I will trust You with all my heart and lean not on my own understanding while acknowledging You and allowing You to direct my path. Thank you in advance for healing and restoring me.

In Jesus' name. Amen.

ABOUT THE AUTHOR

SHERA YNEZ SMITH is a single mother of three beautiful children– Jordan, age twenty-two, Jillian, age eighteen, and Jonathon, age thirteen. She has been married and has experienced a lot of trials and tribulations to help her write this. She is a licensed cosmetologist, instructor, and certified trichologist, which also inspired her to write. Shera is a mentor of many and a woman after God's own heart. Shera is passionate in what she loves, which is to help people with her "being a better you" philosophy. She is the founder, owner, and operator of her first hair loss clinic and natural hair salon in her area.

If you would like to know more about Shera Ynez Smith, she is available for booking. Contact Holistic Aesthetics Inspiring Restoration Center Inc. at 870-819-6556 or 870-351-3740.

J. Kenkade
PUBLISHING®

Our Motto
"Transforming Life Stories"

Also Available from J. Kenkade Publishing

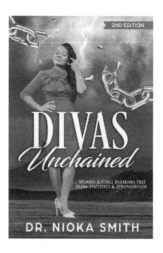

ISBN: 978-1-944486-25-9
Visit www.drniokasmith.com
Author: Dr. Nioka Smith

Sexually abused by her father at the age of 14, pregnant at the age of 17, and a nervous breakdown at the age of 28, Dr. Nioka Smith's painful past almost killed her, until the voice of the Lord guided her into destroying strongholds and reversing Satan's plan for her life. DIVAS Unchained is the powerful chain-breaking reality of the many unfortunate strongholds our women and girls face. Dr. Nioka uses her divine gift to help women and girls break free from destructive life cycles and prosper in all areas of life. Satan has lied to you. It's time to expose his lies. It's time to break free!

Also Available from J. Kenkade Publishing

ISBN: 978-1-955186-02-5
Visit www.amazon.com
Author: Indigo Manning

In this life, there are certain burdens a godly woman will inevitably face. Indigo Manning has seen firsthand how real those burdens can be, but her testimony is that there is joy to be found in serving our Creator because He does not intend for us to shoulder those burdens on our own. When we cast our cares upon Him and ground ourselves in the purpose He has instilled in all of us, we are able to flourish as mothers, wives, sisters, and friends. Perhaps more important than all of those relationships, however, is a woman's relationship with herself. Though trials may come, if we all do the work of self-reflection and personal stewardship, we can maintain identities rooted in Christ and allow the Holy Spirit to work through us.

Also Available from
J. Kenkade Publishing

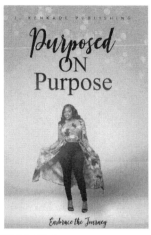

ISBN: 978-1-955186-03-2
Visit www.amazon.com
Author: Janice Buckley

Scripture does not say "yesterday's" faith or "tomorrow's" faith. It simply says "now" faith. Right now, immediately! With faith the size of a mustard seed, you can move mountains. God has given us the same power and authority to speak and see the manifestation thereof. What better time than now to start doing what God has called you to do? What are you waiting for?

You have so much inside of you. You are amazing, and there is no limit on what God has for you. In these chapters, you will discover how I found my Purpose by pursuing God and how on this journey God turned my trials into testimonies that will save lives.

Also Available from
J. Kenkade Publishing

ISBN: 978-1-944486-00-1
Visit www.amazon.com
Author: Donny Blumingburg

Genesis 1:26 (KJV) "And God said, Let us make man in our image, after our likeness: and let them have dominion over the fish of the sea, and over the fowl of the air, and over the cattle, and over all the earth, and over every creeping thing that creepeth upon the earth."

We must understand that we are here on the earth to rule. Not rule over people but we are here to manage the earth and its problems. God has placed in us solutions. There is a problem on this earth that you are meant to solve once you discover that problem. Then, God wants to raise you up, and equip you to be His problem solver. Come on this journey with me of discovery and deeper meaning and fulfillment in life.

Made in the USA
Columbia, SC
25 January 2022